Published by
MAGINATION PRESS
An Educational Publishing Foundation Book
American Psychological Association
750 First Street, NE
Washington, DC 20002

For more information about our books, including a complete catalog,
please write to us, call 1-800-374-2721, or visit our website at
www.maginationpress.com.

Editor: Kristine Enderle
Art Director: Susan K. White
Printer: Worzalla, Stevens Point, Wisconsin

Library of Congress Cataloging-in-Publication Data

Ford, Melanie.
My parents are divorced too : a book for kids by kids /
by Melanie, Annie, and Steven Ford, as told to Jann Blackstone-Ford ;
illustrated by Charles Beyl.— 2nd ed.
p. cm.
ISBN 1-59147-241-5 (hardcover : alk. paper)
ISBN 1-59147-242-3 (pbk. : alk. paper)
1. Children of divorced parents—Juvenile literature.
2. Divorce—Juvenile literature. 3. Remarriage—Juvenile literature.
4. Stepfamilies—Juvenile literature.
I. Ford, Annie. II. Ford, Steven. III. Blackstone-Ford, Jann.
IV. Beyl, Charles, ill. V. Title.
HQ777.5.F67 2006
306.874'7—dc22   2005028423

10 9 8 7 6 5 4 3 2 1

My Parents Are Divorced Too

A BOOK FOR KIDS BY KIDS

SECOND EDITION

by Melanie, Annie, and Steven Ford
as told to Jann Blackstone-Ford

illustrated by Charles Beyl

MAGINATION PRESS • WASHINGTON, D.C.

CONTENTS

1
Learning About the Divorce

When Something Is Wrong

When Parents Divorce

When It's Time to Feel Better

2

Adjusting to Your Parents' Divorce

When Families Change

When Parents Aren't Around

3
Dating, Remarriage, and New Families

When Parents Date

When Parents Get Married Again

Hello! Our names are Melanie, Annie, and Steven. When we were younger, our parents got married. It's a little confusing, but what we mean is that Annie's mom and Melanie and Steven's dad got married to each other. So we're all in the same family now.

When Annie was a baby, her mom and dad got divorced. She was their only child. She lived with Jann, her mom, after the divorce but visited her dad a lot. Then Jann met Melanie and Steven's dad, Larry. And they got married. Annie stays with her dad every other weekend, but she mostly lives with her new family—Jann, Larry, Melanie, and Steven.

Then there is another part of our family. Melanie was four years old and Steven was two when their mom and dad split up. They spent equal time at their mom's house and dad's house, in joint custody. When Larry and Jann got married, Melanie and Steven started switching every other week between their mom's house and their dad's house.

You'll hear all about our families as we tell our stories in this book. But first we want you to know why we wrote this book. We wrote it because we know exactly what it feels like when parents get divorced. We know what it is like when they don't get along and argue about everything!

We understand what it is like when you have to move because your parents don't want to live together anymore or when you have to explain to your friends that your parents split up. We know what it is like when your mom or dad starts to date and then gets remarried. We know that divorce can be very confusing. And we want to help.

Each chapter in this book is divided into sections about different things like dealing with arguments, talking about feelings, missing a parent, or moving to a new house. We also get into parents' dating, remarriage, and new relatives. In each chapter section, we've listed some specific questions and answered them in a way that makes sense to us and hopefully to you too. It's written like this so that you don't have to read the entire book if you don't want to. You can just look at what interests you and get our advice. Let's say you're worried that the divorce is your fault, or you want to learn ways to make yourself feel better when your family is going through problems. If you look in the Table of Contents at the beginning of the book, you'll see that's all in chapter 1, so just thumb through the first chapter and see what we think.

We hope that our stories and advice will help you figure out ways to deal with what is bothering you the most. Everything we have mentioned in this book is true. It all really happened to our family and friends. And some of it may even sound familiar to you. We hope that this book helps. Good luck!

—Melanie, Annie, and Steven

1

Learning About the Divorce

Parents sometimes argue quite a lot and don't get along before they decide to break up. Or as things get bad, parents may even ignore each other. Or your family might not spend time doing stuff together. Whatever is happening, kids almost always know something is wrong before their parents actually tell them. You can just feel it, right? You might not understand exactly why your parents argue or how this could be happening in your family. It could be for a million different reasons!

We always hoped that things would get better in our families, but they never did. At first we worried that maybe it was our fault when our parents argued. Was it because Melanie didn't clean her room? Were they mad because Annie didn't do all her homework? After a while we realized that our parents' problems were not really ours to figure out.

Also we realized that everyone reacts differently to problems. Our parents argued. Melanie got an upset stomach, Annie didn't sleep well, and Steven didn't say anything. But mostly we just didn't feel okay. So when our parents divorced, we had to learn how to deal with all the changes that divorce brings by being honest, talking about feelings, and figuring out ways to make ourselves feel better.

When Something Is Wrong

Melanie: Parents think you're only a little kid and you are not old enough to understand their problems or what divorce means. So they don't take the time to explain.

And the thing is that even if parents aren't arguing in front of you, you can tell when something is wrong or that they don't like each other anymore. Kids understand more than parents think they do.

Annie: When I didn't understand what was going on, my mom explained to me that sometimes kids might not understand some of the things that their parents disagree about. So to protect their children from getting confused or frightened, sometimes parents don't talk about their problems with their children. You know, things like money or problems with their job, stuff like that. Parents think those are adult problems, and most of the time they are right!

My mom told me not to worry about these things. But if I wanted to ask her anything, she promised to answer all my questions as best she could. That helped.

Melanie: Fighting is the worst! My parents didn't think I heard them argue, but I did. I remember they would go into the bathroom and just yell at each other really loud. My bedroom was right outside the bathroom. I would sit on the bed and listen to them. I was only four and it really scared me. I didn't tell them I could hear their arguments because I was afraid to tell them.

Annie: I didn't like it when my parents argued either. I never said anything because I was always afraid my dad would get mad at me if I did. He has a real loud voice, and it scared me sometimes. I didn't know what to do.

Steven: But there is something you can do. You can talk to your parents. You can say, "I don't like it when you and Dad fight." Or "How come you argue with Mom all the time? I don't understand." And maybe that would make some of the arguments stop.

Melanie: But you know, it's hard to talk to your parents when you think they might get mad at you. But whatever! Now, I would just ask them, "What's going on?"

Annie: Yeah, now I would say, "Hey look. I hate it when you fight. It makes me feel real bad!"

Melanie: That's right. Try to talk to your parents and tell them how it makes you feel. Tell them you don't like their fighting.

When Parents Divorce

Annie: Actually, one time I looked up divorce in the dictionary, and it said that divorce is legally ending a marriage contract between a husband and wife.

Steven: Yeah, like the husband and wife are no longer married, but really they have just stopped being married, kind of like it never happened.

Annie: But what it really means to me is that your mom and dad won't be living together anymore. Sometimes one of them moves very far away or sometimes they move just around the corner. But your whole family doesn't live in the same house together anymore.

Melanie: I knew my parents were getting a divorce, but I didn't get what divorce meant. I didn't really understand what was happening until later. When my mom, Steven, and I moved out of our house, it hit me that my dad wasn't coming with us. I found out really quick how things were changing.

Steven: See, it is so important for parents to really explain and for kids to ask questions if they don't understand. I'm not saying that you need to ask your parents about the personal stuff. At first you can ask questions about where you're going to live or where your other parent will be living. Stuff like that. I'd try not to worry about why they were getting divorced or why they didn't want to live together anymore.

I feel like the only kid alive whose parents are divorced. Is it just me ?

Melanie: I've heard that something like almost half of the marriages in the United States end in divorce. And then I think like half of those divorced people get remarried.

Steven: Whoa, that's a lot!

Melanie: So lots of kids and families go through divorce. Families can change like ours did. The trick is to figure out how to deal with divorce and all the changes that follow. And it's not easy. I never thought my parents would get divorced. I had no idea what that even meant! What kid would?

When my parents started arguing a lot and things started feeling weird, I thought my parents would fix things like they always did with everything else. I never thought they would split up. I thought they could solve anything.

Grown-ups always seem to have all the answers. I didn't know any better. Their problems were too big to fix, I guess, so they decided that they couldn't live together anymore and the solution was to get divorced.

Annie: Lots of my friends' parents are divorced too. Some friends live with their moms. One lives with his dad. I have a friend who lives with his grandparents. I have two other friends who live one week at their mom's and one week at their dad's, like Melanie and Steven do. I live with my mom and Larry most of the time. I see my dad every other weekend.

Melanie: I know my parents must have told me they were getting a divorce, but I don't remember. I am sure I didn't really understand anyway because I was only four, but they should have made me understand. I have asked my dad about it, and he said that my mom explained everything to me. But even if I said I understood, I didn't. And getting older didn't help. I had a lot of problems dealing with it. They should answer you every time you ask, even if they think they've already told you. They shouldn't be afraid to talk to you about it.

Annie: My mom and dad were divorced when I was only a baby. I never really lived with them together anyway. My mom got married again when I was three. When I was six, my mom and stepdad got a divorce. That time my mom explained everything to me so I understood. Sometimes stuff still comes up, and I have to ask questions again.

It's important for parents to explain things until you get it and not get mad if you ask them the same questions over and over. Even now, sometimes I think I get what my mom means, but then I think about it and I really don't, so I have to ask her to explain it again. I've learned that that's okay.

Steven: I was only two when my parents got divorced. I don't think anyone explained anything to me because they thought I was too little. But even a little kid can understand, you know? I wish they had tried to explain it to me in a way I could understand, and not be afraid of upsetting me.

Annie: When my mom was married to my stepdad, I had a stepsister, Veronica. He didn't tell her anything when we left. She was five years older than me. I was very close to her. She told me that after we left, she went to her dad's house expecting to see my mom and me, and we were just gone. All her dad told her was that we moved out because he and my mom were getting a divorce. Nothing more! And she was 12! He didn't even try to explain or help her understand.

So Veronica decided to ask her mother what happened and where we were. She hoped her mom would know and clear up the mystery. As things turned out, her mom told her where we were. But Veronica was very mad at her dad, because she felt like he should have explained better. It took Veronica a year to get up enough courage to ask her dad about it.

When she finally did talk to her dad about it, do you know what he said? He didn't think it was that important to her! Can you believe it? You always think that grown-ups are smarter than that, you know?

When she finally came to visit us two years later, my mom talked to her for a long time and explained what happened. She was still so mad at her dad that she was shaking when she told me the story. I told her she had to tell her dad how mad she was. She said she was afraid to talk to him, and she didn't think he would listen to her anyway. She felt that he really didn't care how things looked to her. It bothered her for a really long time. It made her not like her dad that much.

Maybe in a year or so my parents will get back together. Does that ever happen

Steven: Well it could, but don't count on it!

Annie: The truth is that your parents are getting a divorce because they want one. And no matter how bad it is at home, most kids don't want their parents to get divorced. It feels unfair sometimes, but kids have to do what their parents want. I always thought my parents would get back together. I thought that even when my mom got married again she'd change her mind and get back together with my dad.

Melanie: Everyone I have ever talked to who has divorced parents has told me that at some time or another they wished their parents would get back together. They hoped something magical would happen and all the bad stuff would go away and everything would be fine again. I know it was just wishful thinking on my part. Inside I knew my parents would never get married to each other again. They were much happier after the divorce. I just missed my family and wanted things to be like before. I liked my mom and dad and brother all living in one place, and it wasn't like that anymore. That made me very sad.

Annie: I really believed my parents would get back together. Even when my mom was married to someone else, I still thought they might get back together. But I know my parents are happier the way it is now. And I know they both love me. I am happy too. But still, sometimes I wish they weren't divorced.

Melanie and Steven: Yeah.

Melanie: No matter how long your parents are divorced, you sort of wish they would get back together. That's okay. It is totally normal to want that.

Is there anything I can do to stop this divorce from happening?

Steven: One day I was playing with a friend, and he told me he was afraid his parents were going to get a divorce. He thought maybe if he was good and didn't make his parents mad, they might not get a divorce.

He thought it was his fault. I told him it wasn't, that it never is the kid's fault. He didn't really believe me. He thought his parents fought because he was bad. He blamed himself.

Melanie: I never thought that. I just didn't want the divorce to happen.

Annie: I guess it doesn't matter what we do. We can't stop it. Divorce isn't the kids' fault, and we can't do anything to make them stay together.

When It's Time to Feel Better

Annie: I felt it was my fault when my mom and stepfather got a divorce. I don't even know why. I just did. I thought the fighting was my fault. I thought maybe something I did or said was the problem. I thought their problems were my fault. Everything!

My mom said the divorce wasn't my fault, and she told me that she and my stepfather were getting a divorce from each other, not from me. That made me feel a little better.

Melanie: I think kids blame themselves because they don't really understand what's happening. Sometimes parents don't tell you exactly what's happening, or they think we are too young to understand. Sometimes they just leave a lot of stuff out, which makes things confusing.

Annie: Yeah, sometimes a kid can feel left out of the whole thing, and that adds to the feeling that the divorce is really the kid's fault. You're not part of your parents' discussions. You're left out of big decisions.

So if you aren't involved in deciding about the divorce, you might feel like you're not important in the family. Of course, that's not true, but your parents never ask you if you want them to get divorced.

Melanie: First things first. You have to figure out what you're feeling and learn how to talk about it. My parents used to get in big arguments before they got divorced. When they argued a lot, I would get really bad stomachaches. I would try to go to school, but my teacher would send me home because my stomach hurt so much.

My mom took me to the doctor because I had so many stomachaches. The doctor couldn't find anything wrong with me. Nobody ever thought that I got stomachaches and felt sick because I was upset that my parents were fighting. I didn't even know myself. But now I know that I can't keep my feelings inside. I should have tried to talk to my parents and tell them how it made me feel. Keeping everything inside was giving me stomachaches.

Annie: When I was upset, I wouldn't tell anyone. I used to hold everything inside too. I guess that was my way of getting back at the person who made me upset. But I was so angry all the time! I learned that when you hold everything inside, you can end up feeling mad all the time and you can be really mean to people. Of course, I

felt so bad, but I couldn't stop it. Sometimes the anger goes away, but it always comes back.

Melanie: What helped me is that I really needed to figure things out first, before I could talk. My dad used to say I was "labeling my feelings." He meant that I liked to really dig deep and figure out all of my different feelings so I could see what was really causing me to feel that way.

Like if I knew that I wasn't really just mad, but felt stressed out because I didn't finish my homework or felt worried because my mom wasn't around as much as I liked, I could figure out what to do to make myself feel better. It's like finding the real problem and fixing that.

Steven: Sometimes if I felt bad, I didn't know what to say. Problems seemed so big, so I just kept quiet. But if I ignored them, they always came back to bug me.

Annie: Yeah, instead of keeping it inside, you should talk about how you feel. Just start. The words will come. I found out that if I yelled and screamed and acted mad, no one wanted to help. Now I try to explain how I feel and not say, "You always do this or you never do that."

Steven: Annie used to be angry a lot of the time.

Annie: Because I was! I was angry about everything. Now I'm learning to talk about what bothers me. I'm much better than I used to be. I've learned to say things like, "Melanie, I'm angry because you wore my favorite jeans and I was planning to wear them! Please ask before you wear my clothes!" It works. People listen, and I don't like to feel angry inside. I try to tell people when I'm upset. But it's something I had to learn. It doesn't come

naturally. It does with Melanie. She has no problem opening up and telling people why she feels bad. With me it is very, very hard.

Steven: But you're getting better at it.

Annie: Yeah, but it's not easy. I watch Melanie talk about her feelings when she's upset. She thinks about stuff, figures it out, and then tells people how she feels. If they laugh at her or just think she's being a kid, she might still be upset, but it doesn't stop her from telling people what's on her mind. I know it makes her feel better when she gets it all out.

Help! My parents aren't listening. Who else can I talk to?

Annie: I learned if you talk about your problems with someone you feel close to, like a friend, or someone you trust, like a teacher or counselor or another relative, things will stop bothering you. One of my teachers is really cool. I mean, I really like him and he doesn't make me feel stupid if I talk to him. That helps.

Steven: Yep, if you don't think your parents are listening, it's good to talk to someone else. The counselor at my school will see me anytime if I want to talk about a problem. Just getting your feelings out helps so much!

Annie: Yeah, the counselor at school was great, especially when Mom and Larry got first got married. I was part of a group called Changing Families. There were lots of other kids going through the same things, and we all met every week and talked about it. It was good to hear what other kids were going through. Sometimes they had good ideas. And sometimes their stories just made me feel better about our family because we didn't have it so bad!

Melanie: When my friends talk to me about this kind of stuff, I tell them that I know how they feel because I have felt those things too. I tell them that things get better with time, but that I am there for them if they want to talk. For me, talking is what made the difference. Now look at me! I felt very bad before. Now I am just fine.

Annie: Lots of my friends talk to me about their parents' divorce. Most of the time parents are so upset they don't see that their kids are upset too. Sometimes when your parent asks what's wrong, you just say "nothing," because you don't know exactly. You might not even be able to say what's wrong. So parents think everything is fine when it's not.

Steven: You can get in trouble because you're so mad, and you might do stuff you wouldn't normally do. Like my friend Robert. He feels angry all the time. He's always getting into trouble. He never used to before. But he's really upset because his dad just moved out.

Melanie: At school, we also have a special group called the Friendship Group. It's a group of kids who discuss problems together with the help of the counselor. It can be any type of problem, not just problems about divorce.

We would talk and trade stories and work out ways to express our feelings. After I went, I learned that I could deal with my problems even when things felt bad.

Annie: Sometimes kids can't talk to their parents but still need help. When my best friend told me that her stepdad was hitting her mother, I was very upset. We were swimming, and she just started to cry for no reason. She was afraid to tell anyone, because she thought her stepfather might hurt her if she told.

She was very confused. It took us a long time to decide what to do. We decided to ask my mom for help. After we talked to my mom, she called my friend's mom and talked to her. They decided my friend would stay with us for a few days while her parents worked it out. Her parents decided to get a divorce.

Melanie: If you are being hurt or you're afraid of being hurt, you have to tell somebody! There is always someone you can tell. Or if you're embarrassed to tell a friend, then tell your teacher or a counselor or an aunt or uncle. Just tell someone. If you feel afraid, it's a sign that you need help.

Annie: There are lots of things you can do if you don't want to talk. I have a friend who writes in a journal and others who email each other. I have one friend who found a pen pal in Mexico to write to. That helped her. You could also express yourself or work out your problems by writing poems, drawing, dancing, or even playing an instrument. Anything to help you deal with your feelings.

Steven: Any kind of exercise can help you feel better, like just riding your bike.

Annie: Yeah, my friend Abby said she got through her parents' divorce because of playing soccer. She said it felt good to be out of the house playing hard, and she liked being with her team.

Melanie: My friend Sarah's family used to have family movie night. It was a special family thing that they had been doing since she was little. She and her brother Joey got to take turns picking out the movie. They would order pizza and make popcorn and pile up on the couch together. She loved it.

But when her parents split up, movie night stopped. She really missed it. So she asked her mom if they could start it up again. Of course her mom said yes. She hadn't realized how important it was to her. I think movie night gave Sarah something to look forward to and gave her something to hold on to when everything in her family had changed.

Steven: Me, I like to play basketball. Just shooting hoops by myself or with friends. Or maybe I would skateboard around the neighborhood. That sometimes helps me feel better when I am super-stressed and need a break from talking and thinking about stuff all the time.

Annie: I also like reading books or magazines for fun. If I am looking for info on divorce, sometimes I surf the web. Good information is out there that can help or offer advice. I just type "kids and divorce" into Yahoo or Google or some other search engine. That way you can find stuff just for kids.

Adjusting to Your Parents' Divorce

You're right. Adjusting to your parents' divorce is tough. One of the scary things about your parents getting a divorce is that you worry about what will happen to you. Where will you live when your parents no longer live together? Will you live with your mom or dad? And if you choose to live with your mom or decide to live with your dad, will your choice hurt your other parent's feelings? Will you go to the same school? Will you have to leave your friends too? Why does everything have to change?

We felt so much better after we understood how things would be changing and how everything would fit together. We asked our parents questions again and again, and realized that many important things such as always seeing our mom and dad, and going to the same school, would stay the same. That helped a lot.

But we know that some kids don't get to stay in the same house and do have to change schools, and that just makes dealing with your parents splitting up even more difficult. We can only tell you that once we figured out how important it is to tell our parents how we felt and what was bothering us, we felt more in control, less afraid, more secure, and better able to deal with these big changes.

When Families Change

Melanie: I didn't understand why I had to leave my house and my room. Even though we moved only a mile away, I still had to leave my room and my dad. My parents were the ones getting the divorce, not me. So why did I have to leave?

Annie: My mom and I moved two hours away from our old house. It was a lot different from where I used to live. We moved away from my stepfather. I didn't like him that much, so I wasn't sad to go. I felt like I could start all over. I missed my old friends, but I made new friends real fast.

Steven: I was so young I don't remember moving out.

Annie: Moving doesn't have to be that bad. At first, I didn't want to move. My mom asked me to give it a chance and then see how I felt. I did give it a chance, and I liked it much better.

That's what I tell my friends to do. If you really don't like it, then you have to tell your mom or dad and maybe they can change something. They probably won't live together again, but maybe they could help you like the new place better. Also, you can set aside a day after you move to explore the town and find cool things about your new place.

Melanie: When my parents first separated, my mom, Steven, and I moved just a mile away from my dad. My mom and dad share custody of us kids. So we stayed in our old house with my dad, and we lived in a new house with my mom. Mom's house was a lot smaller than Dad's house was.

Steven and I had to share a room there. In the beginning, we switched back and forth every day. That was hard because I had to pack up every day to go to the other place, and it was very confusing. When I was in third grade, sometimes I left my homework at the other house. I even got behind in school.

When my dad got married again, we decided to switch houses every week. I like that better because I still see both my parents, but now I know where I will be. We switch on Fridays after school. That gives us two days to get organized before school starts again on Monday. And we each have a room at both houses!

Steven: One thing I have never gotten used to is having to be so organized. Sometimes I forget my gym shoes at Dad's or my bathing suit at Mom's. That really bugs me. My mom made me a checklist that I can look at before I leave each house, and that has really helped.

Annie: I didn't like going from having a big room all to myself to having to share a room with Melanie. At first it was fun, but then I didn't feel like I had a place of my own. We even had to share a closet. We wore the same size and a lot of our clothes were the same. Everything got all mixed up.

I missed my old room with my own stuff, so my mom let me decorate one wall of the new room all by myself. She didn't care what color I painted it. It was my wall, and I could change it any time I wanted.

Melanie decorated a wall too. We each got to pick out our own comforter so we would feel like we had our own place. Then we moved around the corner to a bigger house and we got our own rooms.

Melanie: I'm not sure you are ever happy all the way with where you live after your parents divorce. Things happen and you wish you were at the other house. Like when we go to my mom's for the week, I always feel like I'm going to miss something at my dad's.

Once I was riding my bike around the neighborhood and saw my dad driving away from our house. We caught up with each other and there was Annie sitting in the front seat. My dad, Jann, and Annie were all going to a baseball game! I had to stay at my mom's because it was my week to live with her.

I was upset at first. But sometimes I go to places with my mom too, so I guess it all evens out. But it takes a while to get used to that.

Annie: I worried that I would lose my old friends when I moved. So I write to my friends. We write back and forth all the time. I really love to get email! I added all my old friends to my email buddy list. We instant message each other sometimes too. It makes it really easy to stay in touch. Also I have a web cam, and it lets me see my friends and my dad. That's cool because I don't live with him all the time.

My old friends come visit me in the summer. We still write, and they always come to stay with me for a few days. Sometimes even their moms come. We all have a great time.

Melanie: My friend Jill moved here after her parents got a divorce. She liked her old house better. She talked about it all the time. Now she's used to living here, but it's been two years. Sometimes it takes a while to see what's cool about a new house. And sometimes it's not really the actual house or moving to a new neighborhood that is bugging you, but instead it's just getting used to the idea that your parents split up, and everything changed.

Steven: Yeah, I know it sounds dumb, and everyone will tell you this, but it really does take time to feel okay with all the changes. You have to be patient, and that's hard! You have to deal with all sorts of things. So just don't try to fix everything at once.

I feel like I am caught in the middle. Do I have to choose between my parents

Melanie: Some kids feel like they have to take sides, but I think that's because they think their parents expect them to. Or their parents might even ask, "Who do you want to live with? Mom or Dad?" I would hate it if I had to choose where I was going to live. What would I say? Either choice would make you feel like you're hurting someone. I think it stinks when parents do that to their kids.

Steven: I remember a time when my parents were not getting along. They were already divorced. I was around four or five years old. My mom wanted to do something she knew would make my dad mad, so she told us not to tell him. Even though I was little, I knew that was wrong. I felt awful.

Melanie: My mom didn't think of it this way, but when she asked us not to tell our dad, it felt like she was asking us to choose which parent we liked best, when we actually loved both our parents the same. If we liked Mom best, we would keep the secret. If we liked Dad best, we would tell him the secret. It was so unfair!

Steven: I was very upset about this, and I had a hard time keeping the secret. Then one day I slipped and told our stepmom. I was glad I told. She called my mom and they worked it out. I don't even remember what it was now. I just know how bad it made me feel to have to keep a secret from my dad.

Melanie: The next time I saw my mom, I told her how it felt to have to keep something from my dad. My mom said she would never ask us to do that again. She didn't realize she was asking us to lie. She just didn't look at it that way. I hated having to choose between my mom and my dad.

Annie: I'll tell you something that made me feel like I had to choose between my mom and my dad and I didn't like it one bit. When I would go to visit my dad, he would say mean things about my mom and where we lived. I love my new family and new house. It made me feel very uncomfortable, and I didn't want to go see him anymore. I told my mom how bad it made me feel, and my mom asked me how I wanted to handle it. We talked for a while and then decided that we would write my dad a letter and explain how I was feeling. I knew he would read the letter and think about things. Then after he got the letter, we could all discuss it. So that's what we did. And it worked. He doesn't do that anymore.

Melanie: Another thing some parents do is they ask the kids what's going on at the other parent's house. That might make you feel like you're spying or telling secrets. "Did your mother get a new car?" "Is your dad dating someone new?" That's just not fair. I would try not to get mad and just say, "Please don't ask me. I don't know. Ask them!"

Annie: Oh, and I hate it when I'm going to visit my dad, and my mom tells me to tell my dad something! She would say, "Tell your dad blah blah blah." What if I explain something wrong? And it's not my job anyway. I would make my mom tell him instead.

Can things get worse after my parents' divorce?

Melanie: I can tell you something that is bad about divorce. Splitting up didn't always stop my parents from arguing. How weird is that? Didn't they get divorced because they couldn't work out their problems and get along? So if the divorce doesn't stop the fighting, what's it all for? Why did we go through this? Even after the divorce, I always get the same feeling when my parents fight. It doesn't matter if they are married or divorced. You don't want them to fight. Ever!

Sometimes this happens to my friends too. If they ask me what to do, I tell them to try to ignore the arguing, because it just makes you feel worse if you think about it all the time. And sometimes it might just go away anyway.

My parents have been divorced for eight years now, and they don't fight at all anymore. As a matter of fact, my parents are really good friends. That makes it easier for me to be around them. But in the beginning, it wasn't like that and I hated it. They fought every time we got picked up to switch houses or whatever. I am so glad they got smart about it. I think they saw how unhappy they were making us, Annie included.

Annie: Something I don't like is that sometimes people whose parents aren't divorced talk about you like you're weird or something. They don't understand at all.

Melanie: My mom took us to the taping of one of my favorite television shows, and they asked for families in the audience to be volunteers. They said you had to have a mom and a dad to be on the show. Because my parents are divorced, my dad wasn't with us and they picked the family behind us.

It made me feel like some kind of freak, like I used to feel when my parents first got a divorce. I didn't like that feeling at all.

I also remember one time my mom and stepdad Jeff went to Chicago to visit his parents, my new grandparents. They live in a beautiful place with a lake and lots of kids.

I was talking about Jeff to a bunch of the kids, and they started to tease me because I called my stepdad by his first name. I tried to explain to them that he's my stepdad and I call him Jeff.

They made me feel like I was weird because my parents are divorced. I got really embarrassed. I guess not many people where they live were divorced, so it seemed strange to them. But where I live, lots of people are divorced. They didn't understand that. They just made fun of me.

Annie: See, that's what I mean. That kind of stuff.

YOU'RE SO LUCKY YOUR PARENTS ARE DIVORCED

EVERY HOLIDAY YOU GET TWICE AS MUCH STUFF AS EVERYONE ELSE!

TRY HAVING TWO TURKEY DINNERS, TWO BOWLS OF YAMS, TWO HELPINGS OF ONION CHEESE SURPRISE, SMILING AND SAYING "NICE TO SEE YOU" TO TWO DOZEN RELATIVES, HAVING TWO GREAT AUNTS, WHO ALWAYS PINCH YOUR CHEEKS, AND TWO HOURS OF RIDING IN A FULL MINI VAN FEELING CARSICK?

Holidays feel so weird. Why can't we all be together?

Annie: For me, one of the worst things about divorce is splitting the holidays between parents. I hate splitting holidays. It is terrible. I hate spending Christmas Eve at one parent's house and Christmas Day at the other's.

I would like to see both of my parents on every holiday, and Melanie and Steven too! I would like us all to be together. Everyone I love in one place. It's another thing when you have to pick where you want to be and I want to be in both places!

Steven: Just getting the divorce is bad, but it feels really bad especially around the holidays. First you miss one of your parents. Then the other. I used to miss Annie when she'd go visit her dad.

Melanie: Yeah, when Annie spends the holidays with her dad, it feels weird. I know she should spend time with her dad. But if she's not around on the holidays, I feel like something is missing.

Annie: So we decided to have a special day after Christmas when we exchange presents between us. In the years that I'm with my dad, the night I come home is the special day. We are always out of school during that week, so we stay up late and open our presents. It's something to look forward to, even after Christmas is over. Melanie and Steven's mom always lets Mel and Steve come over, even if they are supposed to be at her house, but she lives close by My dad lives farther away.

When Parents Aren't Around

It's not fair. Why doesn't my mom spend more time with me?

Melanie: Right after my mom and dad got a divorce, I used to see my dad way more than my mom because she went back to work. She never worked that much before. Then when I would go to my mom's house, she always had friends over or she would be on the phone. She wouldn't be with me.

Then she got a new boyfriend and he was always there. I felt very bad because I wanted to be with my mom and I felt like people were always around. Every time I tried to cuddle with her, my little brother would come over and bug us.

So I talked to Jann about it, and she told me to tell my mom exactly how I felt. She said she knew my mom wouldn't want me to be sad. So I sat down with my mom and I told her I didn't see her enough. I told her I felt like there were people around all the time. We were never together, just the two of us.

My mom said she didn't realize I felt that way and she would make a special effort to spend more time with us. She gave me some new pictures to put in my room at my dad's house that reminded me of the good times we've had together. That way I feel like everyone is around me all the time. She also gave me a card I read every time I miss her. It tells me how much she loves me. I still have it! I keep it on my nightstand.

Annie: When I was very little, my mom traveled on business and I stayed home with my stepdad. I would cry because I missed her. It made it worse when I talked to her on the phone because I wanted to be with her. My stepdad was always working, even if we were home, so I spent a lot of the time alone in my room. My mom realized it was a big problem and decided to change jobs so that she could be home with me more often. Now she has a home office and she's home all the time. Plus now I have Melanie and Steven to hang out with and Larry, Melanie and Steven's dad, who loves me. It's much better!

Melanie: My friend Kaitlyn has the exact same problem with her mom as I did when my parents first got a divorce. She feels very bad because her mom is always with her boyfriend. She has no private time with just her. When she talked to her mom about it, her mom said that she was very close to her boyfriend and wanted to be with him. I feel bad for Kaitlyn because she wanted her mom to make special time for her, and her mom didn't. And you know what else? Now her dad has a new girlfriend and Kaitlyn really feels very alone and left out.

Annie: Kaitlyn needs to figure out some way to make her parents realize how bad she feels. Since she tried talking to her mom, maybe she could talk to her dad.

Maybe that would help. I know how she feels though. I was more used to talking to my mom. But when you're at your dad's or your mom just doesn't get it, you have to talk to your dad. And you have to learn to talk to your dad all by yourself and not depend on your mom to tell him how you feel.

Steven: It's important to be able to talk to both of your parents. They need to be there for you when you need them!

I miss my dad. What can I do?

Melanie: I used to miss my mom when I was at my dad's, and I missed my dad when I was at my mom's. At first that wasn't good. My mom and dad and Jann didn't get along, and it was uncomfortable every time Steven and I had to switch houses. Now all the parents get along, so if we want to see the other parent, we just ask and go. We decided to bring some pictures to both houses. So in my room at my mom's, there are pictures of my dad, Jann, Steven, and Annie at Disneyland. And in my room at my dad's, I have pictures of my mom, Steven, and me when we went to San Diego.

Steven: I have a friend, Sam, whose parents got a divorce. He had to live with his father, who lived two hours away, and his brother had to live with his mother. That was very bad. He missed both his brother and his mom!

Now his father has moved back to our town, so Sam lives with his mom and his brother. They can see their father any time they want. It was just too hard the other way. He likes it better now.

Annie: Now if I miss my mom when I'm at my dad's house, I just call her. It used to make my dad mad if I talked to my mom when I was at his house. He said she was invading his privacy when I called her. I think he was just mad that I missed my mom so much. He thought I wanted to be with her more than I wanted to be with him. I wanted to be with him, but I was used to being with my mom.

It was hard not to see or talk to her for days. I talked to him about it and told him it was nothing against him. I just missed my mom. When he understood, he relaxed. That's how we worked out this problem.

Steven: If I was at my dad's and I missed my mom, I would tell Jann. We would call my mom on the phone. If she wasn't home, we would color pictures for her or I would write her a letter.

I couldn't write, but I would pretend or Jann would write the words for me. Then we would walk to the mailbox together to mail the letter.

That's what I did when I was little. But another thing you can do is email your parents when they aren't around. Email is cool too.

Annie: That can be a problem. I remember at first there was never anything to do at my dad's house. I'm the only kid he has. He had remarried and my dad's new wife is nice, but there are no kids around where he lives, so that means no toys, no video games. What am I supposed to do at his house? It was so boring! So I would plan something for when I was going to be there. Anything. Or I would ask if I could bring a friend or something. Plus none of my stuff is there. I just had a bed in the guest room.

So after being really bored for a long time, I decided to bring some of the stuff to his house that I like to do. I like to draw, so I brought some of my art supplies. I brought my GameBoy and some DVDs. I brought the camera I got for my birthday, and we took some pictures of us together.

Pretty soon my dad was drawing with me, watching movies, and taking pictures. It was pretty cool. I wasn't so bored, and I felt more comfortable in the house. ✳

Dating, Remarriage, and New Families

3

You can feel a little freaked out when your parents start dating. You might not even be used to their divorce in the first place. And what if your parents get remarried? What if you don't like your stepparents? What if your stepsiblings are mean or really different than you? And then, what if you find yourself as part of a new family with more parents, more siblings, and more relatives than you could have ever imagined?

It is so easy to feel scared and get frustrated with big changes when everything is out of your control. We definitely felt all of those things. Slowly we learned that it takes a lot of time to make new families work. We came up with some cool ideas to deal with our problems when we were faced with stuff like sharing a room with another kid when we never had to before, or figuring out just how to talk to our parents so they could understand and listen.

You'll see that there are lots of different ways to be a family, and they are all okay. Just keep talking and working together, and you'll figure the best ways out for you.

When Parents Date

Oh no! My mom is dating.
What if I hate her new boyfriend?

Annie: In the beginning right after the divorce, it's hard to like anyone your parents date. And no matter how nice they are to you, it just doesn't matter. It might even make you mad, you know?

You think, "Why do I have to be around you and I can't even be with my own mom or dad?" I tried to be nice to them, but sometimes you just don't want to deal with it.

Melanie: You might not like your parent's dates for lots of reasons. And sometimes, no one seems right. Sometimes it's because you're not used to the divorce and you won't like anyone. It's too soon and you may just hate the thought of your mom or dad with someone new.

Maybe you're afraid that your parent will like the new boyfriend or girlfriend more than they like you. Or you won't like the dates because they are really bossy or don't like kids.

Steven: Sometimes kids are used to the way it is, and then this new person comes in and tries to take over. What would you expect? Kids don't like it. They don't like the new person telling them what to do. No one likes getting in trouble, but especially not with someone who is not your own mom or dad!

Annie: I didn't like Larry at first. It was always just my mom and me. I wasn't so sure I wanted someone else around all the time. Melanie and Steven were always around and that was cool. Larry was nice, but he was always there. Why couldn't I just be with my mom? Once I started to spend more time with him, just him and me without Steve and Mel, I got used to it.

Melanie: The one thing I can tell you is that your parent's new date needs to make sure they don't act like your parent right from the start and try to tell you what to do. Kids will listen only after everyone knows each other better. But if this new person comes in and starts bossing you around, you will so resent it! Kids already have parents. Even if their parents are divorced, they are still their parents.

When Jann and my dad started to date, she never tried to be our mom. She treated us like she treated Annie, but she never tried to be our mom. She was always funny and she was fun to be around. She knew Steven and I loved our mother, and she never put her down. I knew she liked us. I could tell. And I knew she wasn't being nice to Steven and me just because she was with my dad. So that made me like her too.

Steven: If I didn't like someone Mom dated, I would tell her. She would want to know.

Melanie: But what if that didn't matter, Steven? My friend Kaitlyn hates her mom's boyfriend because her mom is never with her anymore. She liked him in the beginning, but now she feels like her mother would rather be with him than her. And when she said something to her mom, her mom didn't seem to care. Then what would you do?

Steven: I guess I'd tell Dad.

Melanie: What would you say to Dad?

Steven: I think I would say that I was not happy because Mom wasn't spending much time with me.

Melanie: Would you act like you were mad?

Steven: No, I would try to stay calm.

Melanie: Really?

Steven: Yes, because if I was really upset, Dad would get upset too. And I wouldn't like that. That would not help much. But it would be better to talk to Mom in the first place. Then Mom would know how I felt, and we could work on the problem together.

Annie: Sometimes there's a reason why you don't like your parent's choice. My best friend Kelly's stepfather told her that he would like her better if she were a boy! He was serious. He wasn't teasing. Once he went fishing and she wanted to go. But he wouldn't take her because she's a girl. When he came home with a lot of fish, she felt left out and sad.

Melanie: When my dad and Jann got married, I was eight, Annie was seven, and Steven was four. We all sat down together and talked about what getting married meant and how things would change after Dad and Jann got married.

Dad and Jann were great. They really wanted us to feel included. We all decided on the date, New Year's Eve. It was a new year and we were starting over, so that's the day we picked. We all got wedding rings at the ceremony. And we celebrate it as our family's wedding date, not just my dad and Jann's anniversary.

Steven: Remember you can always ask your mom or dad what is going on, if they would like to get remarried or if they are planning to. You might be embarrassed to ask about your parent's love life or feel like it's not your business, but it kind of is.

Annie: Sometimes if you let your parents know what you worry about, they might start including you in big discussions or at least let you know when something is up.

When Parents Get Married Again

Annie: Some kids don't like their stepbrothers or stepsisters, and that can be a problem. They never feel comfortable. Sometimes their new stepbrothers and stepsisters are way older or younger than them, and they have nothing in common. But you don't have to like the same stuff to get along. You may not be best friends, and that's okay as long as you figure out how to get along.

Steven: At first we used to get mad at each other. It wasn't because we didn't like each other. Sometimes Melanie and Annie would just bug me.

Melanie: Now we fight, but not any more than other families I know. It has not always been like this. We all had to make adjustments.

Annie: Looking back at the beginning, it doesn't seem that bad now. But I remember we had what seemed to be some big problems. I had never had brothers and sisters. It was always just me and my mom. We spent a lot of time together. Now she was spending a lot of time with me, but also with Melanie and Steven, and I wanted her all to myself. When Melanie or Steven was sitting on her lap, I would sit right on them. This made Melanie very mad at me. Because my mom couldn't have all three of us sitting on her lap, someone would have to get up. Since Melanie was the biggest, it was always Melanie. And Steven and I would just cuddle up on my mom's lap. Mel felt left out.

Steven: If I didn't think I would like my stepbrother or stepsister, I would try to figure out why.

Melanie: I have a friend who is afraid of her stepbrother. He is five years older than she is, and he tried to touch her in a way she didn't like when their parents left them alone. She told me this a while ago. She told me she tried to tell her mom, but her mom didn't believe her.

I can't imagine telling my mom something like that and her not believing me. It would be embarrassing enough just to tell her. I think they finally went to counseling, but it took a long time.

In a situation like this, if parents don't believe you, you have to find an adult who does. Keep telling people until someone helps you.

What if I don't like my stepmom or stepdad?

Annie: I didn't like my first stepdad. He was always mad at me. Why? What did I do? I was only six. So I spent a lot of time by myself. I was afraid to talk to him. I was afraid he would yell at me. Sometimes he acted like I wasn't there. He would do stuff that would get me in trouble. Like the time he took the little piece of chicken instead of the big piece he was supposed to take. My mom always made a little piece of chicken for me so I could finish my dinner. I couldn't finish the big piece of chicken, and he sent me to my room for not eating all my dinner.

That kind of stuff made me not like him much. My mom would feel bad and she would talk to my stepdad about it, and he would get mad and sometimes it would start more fights. I didn't want to be the reason they were mad at each other, so I stopped talking about it.

Melanie: My friend Jessica told me she thinks her stepdad likes his own kids better than her. She never sees her dad, so she feels left out. Now she hates her stepdad. I told her to tell her mom why she is mad at her stepdad all the time, because her mom can't figure out what's wrong. And there is something wrong. But Jessica is afraid to. Her stepdad has a very bad temper.

Steven: If she doesn't say something, it will never get better. She's got to talk to her mom.

Annie: I don't always get along with Larry either, and I'm not sure if it's because he's my mom's husband or if we are just too different or what. I think people just fight sometimes. It's hard to live with new people.

So now I think I would say, "Mom, I have a problem and I need to talk to you about it. It's a very big problem, so don't get mad." Whenever I say, "Don't get mad," my mom knows I'm serious and tries not to get mad. If nothing is said, things will never change.

But one thing I have noticed when I handle it this way is that my mom knows how I feel and she knows how Larry feels, but Larry and I don't know how each other feels. And we are the ones who are mad at each other! So we should really be talking to each other. Sometimes relying on your mom to fix things doesn't fix anything at all. It's kind of up to you to talk for yourself sometimes.

Steven: Sometimes kids won't like anyone. It's not the stepparent's fault. Kids just want their parents to get back together. Also, I think a lot of kids think their stepparent doesn't care about them or what they think.

Annie: If you really hate your stepmom or stepdad, there may be a good reason, so ask your parent for help. It's pretty hard because parents always think they are right. Most kids hate it when there's fighting. So they won't say anything when there is a problem if they think it will cause a fight.

I found that things just got worse when I didn't talk to someone. If the parent you ask for help doesn't listen or understand how important the problem is, tell someone else who could help.

One of my best friends, Angela, has a big problem with her stepmother. She moved away because of it. Her dad thinks it's just because she wanted to go live with her mom, but that's not it.

There's a lot of stuff he doesn't know. Angela didn't get along with her stepmother at all. When her father was not around, her stepmom was really mean to her. She yelled at her and swore at her.

When she told her dad about it, her stepmom lied and said that Angela was lying. Then her dad would believe her stepmom, and he would get mad at Angela. Her dad really had no idea how bad things were when he was at work.

Angela's mom lives in Georgia. I told her to tell her mom and maybe her mom could talk to her dad, because that's what I always do. She said her mom and dad didn't get along either. When they talk, they only fight. She felt all alone. She finally decided to go live with her mom in Georgia just to get away. I miss her a lot. A really bad thing that happened was that she came back to visit for a month this summer and she stayed at a friend's house. Her dad didn't even know she was here!

Melanie: That's wrong, Annie. Her mom should have called her dad!

Annie: I know! I guess her parents just don't talk to each other. She didn't want to call her dad because he would make her stay with him and she didn't want to see her stepmom. Things can get so messed up.

I'm different from my new family in some ways. How can I feel okay about it?

Annie: Sometimes people from different families are different from each other and don't see things the same way. This is a problem that I'm working on with Larry, and it's hard. He's known Melanie and Steven all their lives. They look at things differently than I do. Sometimes he gets mad at me because I don't act like they do.

Like when he teases me. I hate to be teased. It really makes me mad. I hate to be tickled. Melanie and Steven love it. If Larry teases me and I get mad, then he gets mad, and that starts a big fight.

I also like to be by myself and read. Larry, Melanie, and Steven don't really like to be by themselves that much. I'll be upstairs reading, and Larry will want me to come downstairs and watch TV with the rest of the family. I get mad because I don't want him to be mad at me, but I want to stay upstairs and read.

You just have to remember that everyone in your family comes from different places, and you have to let them be themselves. You have to accept their differences.

Melanie: When Annie and I were little, we liked to dress like twins. We liked to look alike. We thought it made us "real" sisters.

As we got older, we realized we're not alike at all, but that's okay. I'm a cheerleader. My friends like to go to basketball games, and we are into sports. Annie's friends are really different. They dye their hair all sorts of colors and listen to totally different music. At school my friends tease Annie. It embarrasses me. I feel like I have to stick up for her all the time.

Annie: Just because we like different things, it doesn't mean we're really that different inside. You can care for someone who is different and likes different things.

Melanie: I know, but our styles are completely different. I know your friends tease you about me too.

Annie: Yeah, they do.

Steven: I hate when people tease me. It really makes me feel bad, but I just ask them how they would feel if I made fun of their sister or brother or mom or dad. Then I just ignore them.

I think you should always stick up for your family. It makes me feel bad when kids tease me, but I stick up for my family and then ignore them.

Melanie: You know what I did? I made sure that when my friends spent the night on the weekends, they got to know Annie. We all sat around and talked or watched TV. Annie is really funny and she makes us laugh.

Then when we went to school, they knew her. Now they smile when they see each other. They don't make fun of her anymore. Sometimes we even hang out together. Getting to know each other made them accept each other more, but it didn't change anyone. Annie and I are still very different.

Annie: This whole thing taught us that we had to stand up for what we believed in, even if our friends disagree. If your friends see that you are serious about something and they are really your friends, they will stop bugging you. You just have to stand up and be strong and deal with it.

Annie: People are always asking, "Melanie isn't your real sister, is she?" People are always asking who belongs to what parent. "Now let me see," they say. "You are Jann's daughter, aren't you? And Steven and Melanie belong to Larry?" Or they say, "Melanie is not your real sister, is she?" Do they even know how those questions make me feel? I don't think so!

Melanie: One time, a friend's mom was introducing me to one of her friends, and she said I came from a broken home. Broken home? I have two really great homes! She obviously just thinks she knows me. It was weird. Why did she have to say anything like that when she introduced me?

Who cares if my mom and dad are divorced? "Um, this is Melanie. She comes from a broken home." What's that about? I would rather they said, "This is Melanie. I think you will enjoy talking to each other." Or "This is Melanie. Both of you really like sports and I think you will have a lot to talk about." I would have liked her to say something nice about me. Broken home is such a weird thing to say when you introduce someone.

Melanie: Some people would call our new family a stepfamily. Others say we are a blended family, which means that our family members mixed together into a completely new family. But we don't call our family either of those things. Instead we call it a "bonus family." We like thinking about our new family arrangement as a bonus, something that sounds more positive than the evil step-mother and stepsisters stuff you read about in fairy tales.

Steven: One big happy family like the kind you see on TV!

Annie: Yeah, right. Our life together hasn't always been a bonus. Not only did we have to learn to deal with our parents' divorce, but we had to learn how to be a family, and that wasn't easy.

Melanie: When my dad married Jann, I didn't like to call her my stepmom because some of my friends don't like their stepparents and they automatically thought I didn't like Jann. That wasn't true, and besides, it just sounded weird to me. I told my mom, and she said she understood.

One day she and Jann were watching one of my basketball games, and they were discussing what to call stepparents. They were teasing about something and said, "You get a bonus with this family. Two sets of parents." That's when one of our friends who was sitting behind them said, "Well, why don't you call yourselves a bonus family? And you can be bonus parents."

We thought that was cool because when you get a bonus, it's something good, not bad. So now we call our stepparents bonus parents. We call our family a bonus family, and Annie is my bonus sister. Way better than "step," I think.

Steven: When I was four, my dad got married again. Then I had two moms. Actually I can't remember not having two moms! The only bad thing I really remember is my mom didn't like me calling Jann "Mom." She told me it made her feel very bad, and that made me feel like I was doing something wrong.

I didn't know what to do. I knew Jann liked me to call her Mom, and I knew my mom hated it. I decided to tell Jann I couldn't call her Mom anymore. I spent a lot of time with her, and my mom was already feeling bad about that. I didn't want my mom to feel worse. When I would slip and call her Mom, I would feel bad.

So we decided to make up a special name just for her. Her real name is Jann, so I call her Jana. Sometimes Melanie calls her Jana too. She likes it because it's her special name, and my mom likes it too. It didn't make that much difference to me. I didn't see what the big deal was.

Annie: That name thing can be a big deal to some parents. I have a friend who calls her stepmom MJ, for "Mother Jennifer." I have another friend who calls her stepmom Mimi, but her real name is Stephanie. And my friend Justin calls his stepdad Buddy. He has since he was two. I call my stepdad my "bonus dad," and I call him by his first name, which is Larry. I always have. It's fine for me.

Melanie: When Jann got pregnant, we were all very excited on the outside. Everyone in the family really wanted the baby.

But inside I was really worried. Everybody told me we were going to have problems. My aunt, my mom, my other aunt—everybody would say, "Just wait until the baby is born. Things will be so different then. Jann will never be able to spend any time with you. Everything will change."

I was really scared because I liked the way things were. I never said anything to anyone. Then my sister Harleigh was born, and we were all so happy. I have more responsibilities now, but nothing else really has changed. Jann makes special time for all of us. I should have just ignored what everyone was saying.

Steven: I was worried too, but I didn't say anything. I didn't like Harleigh much right after she was born. She didn't do anything. I didn't like it when she cried.

Annie: I was very happy Harleigh was coming, but I did have one big problem. I was afraid my mom wouldn't love me as much anymore. I thought maybe because she gets along so well with my bonus dad and isn't married to my dad anymore that she would love this baby more than she loves me. I never said a word, though.

Now that Harleigh is here, I understand that moms don't do that. I should have said something to her and she would have told me, but I was embarrassed. I didn't know.

We were talking one day before the baby was born, and we realized that this baby would be just as much my sister as Melanie's and Steven's. She would be the only one who is related to everyone in the family. She joins us all together.

Melanie: I had another kind of problem with Harleigh. I was always afraid she would like Annie more than me because Annie lives with her all the time and I have to go to my mom's house every other week. I used to worry about it all the time.

Actually, a different thing happened. She missed me because I had to leave. I felt so bad when I left and she cried for me! I didn't know what to do. It was hard to explain to a little kid her age about divorce.

So I talked to her the best I could. I told her I love her. I told her I'd be back. I told her she could call me any time she wants. My mom understood. Even now, sometimes Jann brings Harleigh over to visit when I'm at my mom's house.

I have new grandparents now!
How is this all going to work?

Annie: Sometimes relatives don't understand how important it is to make your new family work after your parents are divorced. They knew only you before, so they forget and leave the new half out. My grandmother used to remember my birthday, but she would forget Melanie's and Steven's. She was nice to them. She would just forget their birthdays.

As time went on she would remember them. But still, on my birthday my grandmother would try to sneak extra money to me or buy me something special. That caused problems.

Steven: That hurt our feelings.

Melanie: That's when you feel like a stepchild.

Steven: You work hard to make your new family work, and sometimes grandparents or aunts and uncles do things that split you apart. And they don't even know it.

Steven: We didn't want to share friends and toys, but most of all we didn't want to share our parents and wished it would just go back to the way it was before our parents divorced.

Melanie: The biggest thing for Annie and me, I think, was that we both had to learn to share. She moved into my room. I had to share it with her. I had a brother and was used to sharing, but not the stuff in my room. She never had a sister or brother, and she wasn't good at sharing.

Annie is way messier than I am. Her stuff was everywhere, and I often got in trouble for her mess. And my stuff didn't feel that special anymore.

Annie was everywhere I was. At school, at home, in our room, everywhere! She was even with my dad when I couldn't be because I was at my mom's. I didn't like that either.

It got to the point where I was mad at her all the time. She was taking all my friends. She dressed the same way I did. She never let me be with Jann. We were all trying to get to know each other, and it was a hard time.

Finally we decided that when Steven and I went to see

our mom, it would be a good time for Annie to be just with her mom too. But now it's different. Time has really helped. A lot of times Annie just comes with me when I go see my mom. They like each other very much.

Annie: We went to counseling, Mel. Remember when you drew those pictures of me and then crumpled them up?

Melanie: That's right! We went to see Brenda, a counselor we go to sometimes. I told her how mad I was at Annie. She helped me get my anger out by using words and drawing pictures.

I drew pictures of Annie, and then I crumpled them up and threw them in the garbage because I was mad at her. Then Annie came in and we drew pictures together. Brenda asked Annie if she was angry with me. Annie started crumpling pictures up too!

I can't remember much more. That was a long time ago. But I do remember that I felt much better after I crumpled up the pictures. Brenda said, "Your parents know why you are angry now and they can do something to help, so you can leave that anger right there in the garbage. Don't hold it in anymore." And that's exactly what I did. So I guess you just have to want things to work.

Lots of times kids are just mad that their parents have found another partner and don't even try to get along. They hate the idea of new people in their family, and they make everyone unhappy. They try to break up their family. They don't say anything to anyone. They are just mad and mean. I was like that. After a while I realized it wasn't making me feel better and it wasn't helping anyone in our family, least of all me!

What helped is when I figured out if I wanted to make

it work, I had to try to think of everyone as one family together. It was important to remember that this is *your* dad and this is *my* mom, but this is *our* family, you know?

If you are mad at each other, you won't think of each other as your family members. You'll think they are your enemy and you won't get along. Then no one will be happy. Not your mom, not your dad, not you.

What else can I do to help this family work?

Annie: Our family made a pact in the beginning that we would not call ourselves a stepfamily. We were just a family, and that has always been very important to me. I like being a member of an extended family.

I also think it's important to realize that there are no set rules on how to make everyone happy after divorce. You have to make things up as you go along.

Steven: Yeah. And if things don't work, that doesn't mean your family is failing. Just try something else.

Melanie: You have to remember that you have two families now and that is not a bad thing. Lots of times kids automatically think that things are bad and choose

sides. You don't have to choose. You can love both your parents and both your families.

I have a mom and stepdad. They are one family, with me and Steven. I have another family with my dad, Jann, Annie, Steven, and Harleigh. Steven is part of both families too. Annie has her own other family. We have lots of people who love us. No one is better than the other. And remember to talk out your problems. You are all in it together.

Steven: Just try to get along. You have to at least try. Another thing we did was to change our last name. Our last name is Ford. Annie's last name is not really Ford. But when everyone in our family had the same last name except her, she felt out of place and decided to use the last name of Ford too. That made us all feel like we were the same family.

Melanie: We have family discussions. That's another way we work out our problems. It doesn't matter what the problem is. We talk about it as a family.

Okay, family discussions. How do we do that?

Melanie: Our family discussions have rules. First, anyone in the family can call a family discussion and we all have to come. If someone calls a family discussion, that means they are upset about something. No one can stay in their room or say they are busy.

You make an appointment and tell everyone in the family, "I'm calling a family discussion for Sunday at 5 o'clock." Then we all sit around our kitchen table. The person who called it explains why. For example, "I'm upset that I'm doing all the dishes and no one else is helping." Then we all try to work out the problem together.

It is not a time for blame, like blaming someone for not doing the dishes. It's a time to look for solutions together. If someone says, "I do the dishes, too!" that's not a solution. A solution would be to assign days that each family member does the dishes, like Annie gets Monday, I get Tuesday, and Steven gets Wednesday.

Another thing, no one can interrupt or laugh. That's rude. No one can lose his or her temper. And most important, our last rule is that no one can leave the table until the problem is solved and everyone agrees. Family discussions really can work!

Annie: Yeah, family discussions work, but Steven always laughs. When things get too serious, he starts to make noises and tries to change the subject. That's just the way he is.

Steven: No, I listen. I like when we have family discussions.

Melanie: Sometimes Dad loses his temper, but he tries not to. Sometimes it takes a few minutes to solve the problem. Sometimes it takes a long time.

You can work out all sorts of problems this way. Lots of things. I'm ten months older than Annie. I'm one grade higher than she is. Sometimes we fight. Sometimes we get so mad, we can't stand dealing with each other. We make everyone in the house so miserable that someone usually calls a family discussion.

Family discussions have helped us figure out that a lot of the time there is another reason why we aren't getting along. Maybe I got into a fight at school with a friend or I'm upset about a class or Annie is mad because of something her dad said. When something else is stressing me out, Annie just bugs me! We take out our frustration on each other. We are getting better though.

Annie: Once our parents called a family discussion when someone got bad grades, and together we made new homework rules. I called a family discussion once because I was upset with Larry. Mom was out of town on business, so we had to wait for her to come home because everyone has to come to the family discussion. Then we worked out the problem together.

Melanie: I've called a family discussion when my dad and Jann were working too hard and I wanted to spend more time with them. They both have home offices, and they didn't realize they weren't paying any attention to us. They were shocked when I told them, and they changed their schedules around.

Steven: Jann calls family discussions when the feeling in the house gets too tense. We all try to figure out what we can do to change it.

Melanie: So if my friends said they hated their new family, I would suggest a family discussion to try to talk it out. It works for us. The main thing is, you get mad when people stop talking to each other or if you hold it inside or yell back. That doesn't solve the problem. You have to remember, there is a way to make things better. You can't just blame family members for doing something wrong.

Is This It?

Adjustments after divorce and remarriage are not easy, and sometimes when things settle down new stuff comes up. You might feel like you are never getting to the end of your problems!

Well, we understand how it feels when a divorce turns your life upside-down. We know that the hurt feelings from a divorce don't go away for a long, long time. A few years have gone by since we began to write this book, and we still don't like to split holidays or be teased about being divorced. It can be a hassle to switch houses and separate your time between your divorced parents. But things are definitely better now, and they will get better for you too.

With time and lots of honesty, we learned to create a way of living and being a family that works for us. We figured out ways to make ourselves feel better, whether that was talking with friends, doing hobbies, emailing, playing sports, reading, or whatever relieved our stress and made us happy. We learned that there are no rules that can make everyone happy and that everyone reacts differently to problems. We learned that if we were determined and cared about each other, we could make our family work. We learned that there are always lots of good solutions to all sorts of differences.

If we could suggest one thing from our own experiences, we would tell you to always tell your parents how you feel. Even if you don't understand why you are feeling bad, tell them. This will give them a chance to help you.

We hope that reading this book has helped too! ✳